FLORENCE BLAKELEY'S FAMOUS RED VELVET CAKE

Episode: "These Games"

Prep time	Cook time	Serves
30 Min	**35 Min**	**12**

- 2 ½ cups all-purpose flour
- 2 Tbsp cocoa powder
- 1 tsp baking soda
- ½ tsp salt
- ½ cup butter, softened
- 1 ½ cups sugar
- 2 eggs
- ¾ cup vegetable oil
- 1 tsp vinegar
- 1 ¼ cups buttermilk
- 2 tsp vanilla
- 1 ¼ Tbsp red food coloring gel

- 2 round 8-inch baking pans
- Cooking Spray

For frosting:

- 12 oz cream cheese, softened
- ¾ cup butter, softened
- 4 cups powdered sugar
- 1 ½ tsp vanilla
- ¼ chopped toasted pecans
- 1 large heart cookie cutter
- 1 disposable decorating bag
- Wilton® #2D piping tip

Sift together the flour, cocoa powder, baking soda and salt in a mixing bowl and set aside. Beat the softened butter and sugar together until fluffy. Add the eggs one at a time. Next, beat in the vegetable oil, vinegar, and buttermilk. Gradually beat in the dry ingredients until incorporated. Stir in the vanilla and red food coloring. Pour batter evenly between two greased 8-inch baking pans.

Bake at 350 degrees for 28-35 minutes or until a toothpick inserted in the center comes out clean. Let cool for 15 minutes and remove from pans and place on a wire rack to cool completely. Level off the tops of the cooled cakes and reserve scraps for garnish. For the frosting, beat together the cream cheese, the butter, and the vanilla. Gradually add the powdered sugar and beat until fluffy. Assemble and frost the cake and decorate the top by placing the large heart cookie cutter in the center and adding the chopped pecans in the middle of the cookie cutter to make a little heart. Press the nuts lightly and remove cookie cutter.

Decorate the top edges of the cake with the #2D piping tip by making rosettes and sprinkle fine crumbles from the cake scraps on top of the rosettes.

ABIGAIL'S SCONES

Episode: "Second Chances"

Prep time	Cook time	Serves
15 Min	**14-17 Min**	**12**

- 4 cups all-purpose flour
- 2 tsp baking powder
- 1 tsp baking soda
- 1 cup granulated sugar
- 1 cup cold butter
- ¼ tsp cream of tartar

- 1 cup sour cream
- 1 tsp vanilla extract
- 2 eggs
- 1 cup raisins
- 3-inch biscuit cutter

Mix sour cream, vanilla, and baking soda together in a bowl. In another bowl, combine the dry ingredients. Cut the cold butter into small cubes and cut the butter into the dry ingredients with a fork. Stir in the sour cream mixture and add 1 egg into the rest of the ingredients. Add the raisins and stir until they are incorporated.

Using a rolling pin, roll out dough on a floured board and fold it in half. Repeat 3 more times and roll dough until it is about ¾" thick. Using a 3-inch biscuit cutter, cut dough out and place on a cookie sheet lined with parchment paper.

Mix the remaining egg and 1 Tablespoon of water to create an egg wash. Brush the egg wash on top of each scone.

Bake 350 degrees for 14 - 17 minutes or until golden.

THE SALOON'S SWEET HONEY CORNBREAD

Episode: "Second Chances"

Prep time	Cook time	Serves
5 Min	**10-12 Min**	**24**

- 1 (8.5 oz) box of Jiffy® cornbread muffin mix
- 1 egg
- ⅓ cup of milk
- ½ cup sour cream
- ¼ cup vegetable oil
- ½ Tbsp sugar
- 2 ½ Tbsp honey
- Cooking Spray
- Mini muffin pan

Mix sugar with box mix in a large bowl with fork, breaking up any lumps.

In a small bowl, mix together egg, milk, sour cream, oil, and honey. Pour into dry mixture and stir until combined.

Spray mini muffin pan with cooking spray. Fill each muffin tin ⅔ of the way full and bake at 350 degrees for 10-12 minutes.

Cool 10 minutes and remove from pan.

ABIGAIL'S CAFÉ
BLUEBERRY PIE MUFFINS

Episode: "Love Comes First"

Prep time	Cook time	Serves
15 Min	**20-30 Min**	**12**

ingredients

- 3 cups flour
- 1 Tbsp baking powder
- 2 eggs
- 1 cup granulated sugar
- ¼ cup brown sugar
- 1 ½ tsp vanilla
- ¼ cup butter, melted
- ¼ cup canola oil
- 1 cup evaporated milk
- 1 ½ cups fresh blueberries
- 1 tsp lemon zest
- 1 (21 oz) can blueberry pie filling
- 1 small heart cookie cutter
- Cooking spray

instructions

Pre-heat oven to 450 degrees and grease muffin pan with cooking spray. Be sure to spray the top of the pan so muffin tops won't stick. Combine flour and baking powder in a large bowl. In a mixing bowl, beat eggs, sugars, vanilla, oil, and butter. Add evaporated milk and mix until incorporated. Stir in the flour mixture, do not overmix. Fold in fresh blueberries and lemon zest. Spoon batter into muffin cups and fill all the way to the top.

REDUCE heat to 350 degrees and bake 20-30 minutes. Pre-heating to 450 degrees and reducing to 350 degrees will create the perfect muffin dome. Let cool completely.

Slice the top off the muffin and cut out a heart shape. Spread a thin layer of blueberry pie filling onto the cut portion of the bottom layer. Place the top of the muffin on the blueberry pie filling. Spoon more pie filling into the center of the heart.

HOPE VALLEY BISCUITS

Episode: "Prelude to a Kiss"

Prep time	Cook time	Serves
10 Min	**15 Min**	**20**

- 2 cups all-purpose flour
- 1 Tbsp baking powder
- ¼ tsp baking soda
- 1 tsp salt
- 6 Tbsp cold butter, cut into small cubes
- 1 cup cold buttermilk
- 2 ½ - inch biscuit cutter

In a large bowl, whisk dry ingredients together. Next, cut butter in using a fork until crumbly.

Pour in buttermilk and stir to combine but do not overmix. Place dough on a floured board and roll with a rolling pin to ¾ inch thick.

Fold dough in half and repeat 4-5 more times. Using a 2 ½ inch biscuit cutter, cut biscuits out and place on parchment paper-lined cookie sheet.

Bake for 13-15 minutes at 450 degrees or until golden. Serve with strawberry preserves.

LEE'S TREE CUPCAKES

Episode: "Trials of the Heart - Part 1"

Prep time	Cook time	Serves
25 Min	**22-28 Min**	**15**

For the cupcakes:
- ¾ cup granulated sugar
- ¼ cup light brown sugar
- ¾ cup plus 2 Tbsp of flour
- 6 Tbsp unsweetened cocoa
- ¾ tsp baking powder
- ¾ tsp baking soda
- ½ tsp salt
- 1 egg
- ½ cup milk
- ¼ cup vegetable oil
- 1 tsp vanilla extract
- ½ cup boiling water

For the frosting:
- ½ cup butter, softened
- ⅔ cup unsweetened cocoa
- 1 ¼ tsp vanilla extract
- ¼ cup milk
- 3 cups powdered sugar - more if needed

For the Decorations:
- Pretzel sticks
- 1 (12 oz) bag of green candy-coating wafers
- Green sugar sprinkles
- 1M piping tip
- Piping bags
- Parchment paper

Heat oven to 350 degrees and line a muffin pan with cupcake wrappers. Combine dry ingredients in a large mixing bowl. Next, add milk, vanilla, oil, and egg, and beat with mixer for 2 minutes. Stir in boiling water, batter will be very thin. Fill cups with batter about ⅔ full and bake for 22 - 28 minutes. Cool completely.

For frosting, beat together softened butter and cocoa until combined completely. Add powdered sugar and milk a little at a time while beating with mixer. Add another tsp of milk - if needed. Mix in vanilla.

For the trees, line pretzels on a cookie sheet lined with parchment paper. Melt green candy coating according to package instructions. Place melted candy coating into a disposable piping bag and cut off a small amount of the tip. Start drizzling the melted candy on top of the pretzel sticks. Start about ½ way up each stick so that it resembles a tree. Sprinkle green sugar sprinkles on top of the tree before they dry. Frost each cupcake with a 1M piping tip and top with a pretzel tree.

THATCHER ESTATE PEACH MELBA

Episode: "Trials of The Heart, Part 2"

Prep time	Cook time	Serves
5 Min	**15 Min**	**6**

- 2 (15 oz) cans peach halves in heavy syrup
- 3 cups fresh raspberries
- ¼ cup powdered sugar
- 1 Tbsp lemon juice

- Vanilla ice cream
- Mint leaves
- Fresh raspberries for garnish

Drain the heavy syrup from the 2 cans of peach halves and reserve ¼ cup peach syrup.

For sauce, add the reserved ¼ cup peach syrup, powdered sugar, 3 cups fresh raspberries, and lemon juice into a blender.

Blend until smooth. Strain out raspberry seeds using a fine sieve. Put one peach half in a small bowl with a scoop of vanilla ice cream.

Top with the sauce, fresh raspberries, and mint.

COULTER'S SNICKERDOODLE SAWMILL MARSHMALLOW RICE TREATS

Episode: "Trials of the Heart, Part 2"

Prep time	Cook time	Serves
10 Min	**24 hours (including decorating and drying time)**	**16**

ingredients

- 6 cups rice cereal
- 4 cups mini marshmallows
- 1 tsp vanilla
- 3 Tbsp butter
- 3 Tbsp granulated sugar
- 1 tsp ground cinnamon
- White fondant
- Brown food coloring
- Vodka or vanilla extract

- Food safe paint brush
- Silver food coloring spray
- 1 ½-inch round circle cookie cutter
- Wilton® #5 piping tip
- Small heart cookie cutter
- ¼ cup dry rice cereal, finely crushed
- Dull knife
- Cooking Spray

instructions

Melt butter over medium heat in a medium saucepan. Pour the marshmallows into the melted butter and stir constantly over medium heat until melted. Remove from heat. Stir in the 1 tsp of vanilla extract. Place 6 cups of rice cereal into an extra-large bowl. Pour the marshmallow mixture over the cereal and stir to coat. Mix thoroughly and press into a 9 X 13" pan coated with cooking spray. In a small bowl, mix together the cinnamon and sugar. Sprinkle the mixture over the top of the cereal. Let cool completely (about 30 minutes) cut into bars measuring 2 inches by 3 inches. Roll out white fondant and cut to fit the top and the two long sides of the treats. Lightly press the fondant pieces to the treat to secure. Using a dull knife, score the fondant so it looks like wood. Mix together the brown food coloring and a little vodka or a little vanilla extract. With

a food safe brush, paint the fondant a light brown. Roll out more fondant and using the circle cutter, cut out a round shape. Using the tip end of the #5 piping tip, cut out a small hole in the middle of the round fondant. Using the pointy end of the small heart cookie cutter, cut out the saw blades around the edges of the fondant circle so it resembles a saw blade. Spray with silver food coloring mist. Let dry completely overnight or for 24 hours. Make a small slice into the end of a treat and press the saw blade into the slit so that it is standing up. Sprinkle the crushed cereal near the saw blade on top of the treat.

ROSEMARY'S
OATMEAL RAISIN COOKIES

Episode: "Follow Your Heart"

Prep time	Cook time	Serves
15 Min	**11-13 Min**	**About 25**

ingredients

- 2 cups flour
- 1 tsp baking soda
- 1 tsp baking powder
- 1 tsp salt
- 1 cup unsalted butter
- 1 cup granulated sugar
- 1 cup dark brown sugar, firmly packed
- 2 tsp vanilla
- 2 eggs
- 3 cups quick cooking oats (not instant)
- 1 ½ cups raisins

instructions

In a large bowl combine the flour, baking soda, baking powder and salt. Whisk together and set aside. In another bowl, beat together the butter, sugars, vanilla, and eggs with a mixer on low speed. Increase speed to medium and cream until fluffy.

Stir in the flour mixture until no flour is visible. Fold in the oats and raisins.

Put 2 Tbsp of dough for each cookie on a parchment-lined cookie sheet. Make sure there is 2 inches between each cookie.

Bake at 350 degrees for 11-13 minutes.

LAURA'S SUNRISE
OVER HOPE VALLEY COOKIES

Episode: "New Year's Wish"

Prep time	Cook time	Serves
25 Min	24 Hours (including decorating time)	**24**

- 1 cup butter
- 1 ½ cup sifted powdered sugar
- 1 egg
- 1 tsp vanilla
- 3 cups sifted all-purpose flour
- 1 tsp baking soda
- 1 tsp cream of tartar
- ½ tsp salt

For the icing:
- 3 Tbsp meringue powder
- 4 cups sifted powdered sugar
- 5-6 Tbsp lukewarm water

For the decoration:
- Edible images
- Light corn syrup
- Food safe paint brush

Cream butter in a mixing bowl. Gradually add powdered sugar and mix until light and fluffy. Add egg and vanilla and mix until thoroughly combined. Sift together flour, baking soda, cream of tartar and salt. Gradually add the flour mixture to the creamed mixture until combined completely. Shape dough into a ball and roll out into a lightly floured surface to ⅛-inch thickness. Cut dough into 2 ½ by 4-inch rectangles. Place on parchment paper lined cookie sheets and bake 10-12 minutes in a pre-heated 375-degree oven or until bottoms are golden. Cool completely. For the icing, place sugar and meringue in a mixing bowl and mix together. Add water and mix low to medium speed with a stand mixer for 7-10 minutes. If using a hand mixer, increase the time and beat until icing loses its sheen. To thin icing to desired consistency, add one tsp of water at a time. Frost each cookie with the icing and let dry overnight. For the edible image, I took a picture of Laura's drawing on my television and transferred it to a Word document. I made multiple images the size of the cookie and went to my local bakery where they printed edible images for me. Most grocery store bakeries will do this for you. Cut out the images and attach to the cookies using light corn syrup. You can always skip the edible image and paint on the scene yourself using food coloring mixed with a little vodka.

FAITH'S INFIRMARY FUDGE

Episode: "A Gentle Heart"

Prep time	Cook time	Serves
20 Min	**Refrigerated Time 4 Hours, Decorating Time 24 Hours**	**25**

- 2 cups milk chocolate chips
- 1 cup semi-sweet chocolate chips
- 1 (14 oz) can sweetened condensed milk
- 1 tsp rum extract
- dash of salt
- White fondant
- Red food coloring marker
- Blue food coloring marker
- Chocolate frosting
- Heart sprinkles
- Mini heart cookie cutter
- Mini round cookie cutter

Spray a 9 X 9" pan with non-stick cooking spray and line it with parchment paper. Place the chocolate, condensed milk and salt in saucepan over medium-low heat. Stir well until smooth. Remove from heat. Add the rum extract and stir to combine. Pour the fudge into the prepared pan smoothing it for an even layer. Place in refrigerator 4 hours or until set. Cut into 25 squares. Roll out white fondant and cut out 12 mini hearts and 13 mini circles. Let dry overnight.

When the fondant is completely dry, make heartbeat lines using the blue food marker in the middle of the heart shaped fondant. Using a small amount of frosting on a toothpick, attach a heart sprinkle underneath the heartbeat line. Using the red food marker, draw a medical cross in the middle of the mini round circle. Attach the fondant hearts and circles to the top of the fudge using chocolate frosting.

KINDNESS WEEK COOKIES

Episode: "A Gentle Heart"

Prep time	Cook time	Serves
30 Min	**30 Min**	**12**

- 1 (12 oz) package white candy coating
- 12 Oreo® cookies
- Yellow fondant
- Black edible food coloring marker
- Red heart sprinkles
- White heart sprinkles

Melt candy coating in microwave according to package instructions. Pour the coating into a deep container and dip the cookie into the coating until completely submerged. Lift out with fork and tap against the container to remove excess coating. Carefully slide the coated cookie onto parchment paper to set.

Roll yellow fondant into 12 (½ inch) oval shaped balls. Draw on bee stripes and two dots for eyes using the black edible food marker.

Attach two white heart sprinkles for wings onto the bee with a toothpick dipped in melted white candy coating. Attach fondant bee to the top of the cookie using melted white candy coating. Attach the red heart onto the top of the cookie on the opposite side of the bee using melted white candy coating.

Let everything dry completely. After completely dry, connect the bee to the red heart with little dashes drawn in with a black edible marker for a bee line.

OPAL'S BROWNIE BITES

Episode: "Hearts in Question"

Prep time	Cook time	Serves
10 Min	**20 Min**	**24**

- ½ cup (1 stick) butter, melted
- 1 cup granulated sugar
- 1 tsp vanilla extract
- 2 eggs
- ½ cup all-purpose flour
- ⅓ cup unsweetened cocoa powder
- ¼ tsp baking powder
- ¼ tsp salt
- Pink buttercream frosting
- 24 teddy bear graham crackers
- Black edible food coloring marker
- Heart sprinkles
- Mini cupcake liners
- Mini cupcake muffin pan

For the frosting:
- ½ cup butter, softened
- 1 ½ tsp vanilla extract
- 2 cups powdered sugar, sifted
- 2 Tbsp heavy cream
- Pink food coloring
- Wilton® #1M piping tip
- 1 disposable piping bag

Heat oven to 350 degrees. Place mini cupcake liners into mini muffin pans and set aside. Mix butter, sugar, and vanilla with a spoon into a large bowl. Add eggs and beat well. In another bowl, whisk together the flour, cocoa powder, baking powder and salt. Gradually add the flour mixture into the egg mixture until completely blended. Bake 20-25 minutes and let cool completely. For frosting, cream butter with mixer until fluffy. Beat in powdered sugar a little at a time until fluffy and completely incorporated. Mix in vanilla and pink food coloring. Add in the heavy cream and beat until fluffy and smooth, about 3 minutes. Frost each brownie with pink buttercream using a Wilton® #1M piping tip. Using the edible black food marker, draw faces on the graham cracker bears. With a toothpick dipped in a little frosting, attach a heart sprinkle to the center of each graham cracker bear.

Place 1 bear on top of each frosted brownie.

HARPER'S SAINT FRANCIS PRAYER STAINED GLASS JELL-O® SQUARES

Episode: "When Calls the Heart Christmas"

Prep time	Cook time	Serves
15 Min	**2 days to set Jell-O®**	**24**

ingredients

- 1 (3 oz) box strawberry Jell-O®
- 1 (3 oz) box orange Jell-O®
- 1 (3 oz) box lime Jell-O®
- 1 (3 oz) box lemon Jell-O®
- 4 cups boiling water
- 2 envelopes (.25 oz each) unflavored gelatin
- 2 cups boiling water
- 1 (14 oz) can sweetened condensed milk

For Decoration:

- 1 (8 oz) container frozen whipped topping, thawed
- White fondant
- Small 1 ½-inch heart cookie cutter
- Green, Red, Yellow, and Orange food coloring
- Edible black food marker
- Vodka or clear vanilla extract
- Food safe paint brush

instructions

For each flavor, dissolve 1 box of Jell-O® in cup of boiling water. Pour into separate plastic sandwich containers and chill overnight. After the Jell-O® has set overnight remove them from the containers and cut them into small blocks using a pizza cutter. Carefully sprinkle the blocks of Jell-O® in a 9 X 13" pan.

In a mixing bowl, dissolve the two envelopes of unflavored gelatin in 2 cups boiling water. Allow mixture to cool. Add the can of sweetened condensed milk stir and cool (make sure that this mixture is completely cool to the touch, so you do not melt the Jell-O® cubes) Pour the cooled milk mixture over the Jell-O® cubes and chill overnight. Cut into squares. For the decoration, roll out fondant and cut into heart shapes. Let dry overnight.

Paint stained glass patterns on heart using food coloring mixed with a little vodka and outline with black edible marker. Write the words, "Love, Hope, Faith" in the center of the hearts. Put a little whipped topping on the Jell-O® square and place the fondant heart on top.

ELIZABETH'S EASY CHERRY COBBLER

Episode: "Words from the Heart"

Prep time	Cook time	Serves
5 Min	**45 Min**	**15**

- ½ cup (1 stick) butter
- 1 cup all-purpose flour
- 1 cup milk
- 1 cup granulated sugar
- 2 tsp baking powder
- 2 (21 oz) cans cherry pie filling

Heat oven to 350 degrees. Place 9 X 13" pan in the oven with the stick of butter until the butter is melted.

Remove pan from oven when butter is melted.

In a bowl mix milk, flour, sugar, and baking powder and pour on top of hot butter.
DO NOT STIR.

Next, pour 3 cups cherries (about 1 ½ cans) on top and do not stir. Bake 45 minutes or until golden.

ROBERT'S
BLACK BEAR COOKIES

Episode: "Heart of Truth"

Prep time	Cook time	Serves
5 Min	**15 Min**	**12**

- 12 Oreo® cookies
- 12 mini vanilla wafer cookies
- 1 (16 oz) container chocolate frosting
- 12 brown M&M's®
- Black edible food coloring marker
- 24 semi-sweet chocolate chips
- 24 candy eyes

Spread chocolate frosting on the back of a mini vanilla wafer cookie and place on top of the Oreo® towards the bottom.

Attach the M&M®, using frosting, to the mini vanilla wafer for the nose. With the black edible marker, draw the mouth on the vanilla wafer under the nose.

Attach two chocolate chips to the top of the Oreo® for the ears with frosting.

Next, attach the candy eyes on the Oreo® above the vanilla wafer.

EMILY'S
CARNIVAL CANDY APPLES

Episode: "The Heart of The Community"

Prep time	Cook time	Serves
20 Min	**20 Min**	**4**

- 4 apples (Granny Smith)
- 4 cups boiling water
- 1 (11oz) bag wrapped caramels
- 2 Tbsp milk
- 4 wooden sticks
- Butter
- Wax paper
- Red fondant
- Small heart cookie cutter
- Rainbow sprinkles

Remove stems from apples. Place 1 apple in the boiling water for 10 seconds. Remove and rub dry vigorously. (This step is critical for removing wax which will allow the caramel to stick. It is important to do this one at a time and not put all of the apples in the boiling water together.) Remove wrappers from all the caramels and place in a microwavable bowl. Add 2 Tbsp milk to the bowl and microwave on high for 1 minute. Remove bowl from microwave and stir. Place bowl back into microwave another minute. Remove and stir. If necessary, heat in 15 second intervals until smooth.

CANDY
APPLES

Place wax paper on cookie sheet and coat with butter. Push a stick in the top of each apple. Dip apple in melted caramel mixture and let excess drip off. Place the bottom of the apple immediately into a bowl of rainbow sprinkles.

Place apple on wax paper. Roll out red fondant and cut out 4 hearts. Place the heart on the front of the apple after caramel has set but is still sticky.

FRACTIONS ARE EASY AS PIE

Episode: "My Heart Will Go On"

Prep time	Cook time	Serves
30 Min	**1 Hour**	**8**

For pie crust:
- ¾ cup shortening
- 2 cups flour
- ¼ tsp salt
- ⅓ cup milk
- Small heart cookie cutter

For pie filling:
- 6 Granny Smith apples
- ¾ cup sugar
- 3 Tbsp butter
- 3 Tbsp flour
- 1 tsp cinnamon

Combine the shortening and milk. Mix in the flour and salt thoroughly to combine. Divide dough into two equal balls. Roll one ball with a rolling pin on a floured surface to about ⅛-inch thickness. Place into a 9-inch (deep dish) pie plate, pressing any air bubbles out and overlap the edge of the plate. Peel, slice and core the apples. Mix the sugar, flour, and cinnamon together in a bowl. Coat the apples in the cinnamon-sugar mixture and put the apples into the pie crust. Sprinkle the remaining cinnamon-sugar mixture over the apples in the pie pan. Cut up the 3 Tbsp of butter and put over the apples. Roll out the other ball of dough to ⅛-inch thickness and place on top of the pie pan. Trim off excess crust and crimp edges. Roll out the excess crust and cut out heart shapes with the cookie cutter. Place the heart shapes on top of the pie in a pretty pattern and make slits in the top crust with a knife. Bake for 45 minutes at 400 degrees. Cover the edge of crust with foil and remove the foil for the last 20 minutes of baking.

TIMMY'S
PEANUT BUTTER PIANO BARS

Episode: "My Heart Will Go On"

Prep time	Cook time	Serves
20 Min	**2 Hours** (including cooling time)	**8**

- ¾ cup granulated sugar
- ¾ cup light corn syrup
- 1 cup creamy peanut butter
- 1 tsp vanilla
- 4 ½ cups Special K® cereal
- 2 cups semi-sweet chocolate chips
- Cooking Spray
- 9-inch heart pan
- 3 white Kit Kat® bars
- 2 dark chocolate Kit Kat® bars

In a medium size saucepan, stirring constantly, bring sugar and syrup to a boil. Remove from heat and add peanut butter and vanilla. Stir until smooth. Put the cereal in a large bowl. Pour the peanut butter mixture over the cereal and stir until well-coated. Press into a very well-greased 9-inch heart shaped pan. Melt the chocolate chips in the microwave and spread over the cereal. Tap the pan to remove bubbles and let cool for about 2 hours. When completely cool, run a knife along the edge of the pan and tip the cereal heart out of the pan and place onto a serving plate.

Place 3 white Kit Kat® bars across the center of the heart for the piano keys. Separate the dark chocolate Kit Kat® bars into sticks and cut ⅓ off the top of each stick.

Place the dark chocolate keys on top of the white keys in the appropriate places on the piano keyboard.

DOTTIE'S DRESS SHOP MARSHMALLOW POPS

Episode: "Heart of a Secret"

Prep time	Cook time	Serves
10 Min	30 Min	12

ingredients

- 12 regular marshmallows
- 12 lollipop sticks
- 1 (12 oz) bag candy coating (any color)
- 12 mini cupcake wrappers
- 12 regular size cupcake wrappers
- A variety of sprinkles, fondant, food coloring spray and/or edible food coloring markers
- Styrofoam® block
- Paper doily and tape

instructions

Melt candy coating according to package instructions. Dip the tip of one end of the lollipop stick into the candy coating. Push in the bottom of the marshmallow and let dry so stick is secure. Using a knife, cut a neckline in marshmallow if desired. Dip the marshmallow into the melted candy coating and tap the stick on the side of the bowl to remove excess candy coating. Place the stick in the Styrofoam® and let it dry completely. With a toothpick dipped in the melted candy coating, attach sprinkles.

Draw on buttons and patterns with food coloring markers. Spray on lace using a paper doily and food coloring mist. Have fun creating your own fashions. Turn the small cupcake wrapper upside down. Poke the lollipop stick in the middle of the cupcake wrapper and push up to meet the bottom of the marshmallow. Secure underneath by wrapping the tape around the stick under the hole so it does not slide down. Repeat with large cupcake wrapper.

ANNA'S HOT CHOCOLATE CAKE

Episode: "Heart of a Secret"

Prep time	Cook time	Serves
20 Min	**1.5 Hours** (including decorating time)	**8**

- 1 cup granulated sugar
- 1 cup light brown sugar
- 1 ¾ cups all-purpose flour
- ¾ cup unsweetened cocoa powder
- 1 ½ tsp baking powder
- 1 ½ tsp baking soda
- 1 tsp salt
- 2 eggs
- 1 cup milk
- ½ cup vegetable oil
- 2 tsp vanilla extract
- 1 cup boiling water
- 1 (.7 oz) packet instant hot cocoa mix
- 1 (8 oz) tub frozen whipped topping, thawed

For the chocolate frosting:

- 1 cup (2 sticks butter), melted
- 1 ⅓ cups unsweetened cocoa powder
- 6 cups powdered sugar
- ⅔ cup milk
- 2 tsp vanilla extract

For Decoration:

- White fondant
- Red Fondant
- Heart sprinkles
- 4 oz white candy melts
- Mini marshmallows
- Parchment paper

Pre-heat oven to 350 degrees. Liberally grease 3 (6 inch) round baking pans. In a large bowl, stir together the sugars, flour, cocoa, baking powder, baking soda and salt. Add the eggs, milk, oil, and vanilla. Beat for 2 minutes at medium speed. Pour the hot cocoa packet into the boiling water and mix until dissolved. Pour the hot chocolate into the batter and stir to incorporate. (BATTER WILL BE VERY THIN) Pour batter evenly into the greased pans. Bake for 30-35 minutes or until a toothpick inserted into center comes out clean. Cool cakes for 15 minutes and remove from pans onto wire racks. Cool completely. For the frosting, stir cocoa into melted butter and alternately add powdered sugar and milk. Mix in vanilla. Assemble cake and frost layers in between. Completely cover the outside and top of cake with chocolate frosting. Roll out enough white fondant to wrap around the entire cake and trim top and bottom to fit. Roll the extra white fondant into a rope about 6 inches long for the cup handle. Shape the rope into a handle and push toothpicks halfway into each end. Allow to dry completely or overnight. Roll out the red fondant and using a 2 ½-inch heart cutter, cut out the shape of a heart. Attach the heart to the front of the cake with a little water. Melt white candy coating according to package instructions. Place the melted candy coating into a disposable piping bag

and drizzle "steam" onto parchment paper. Place in refrigerator to harden completely. Decorate the top of the cake with the thawed whipped topping, the heart sprinkles, the miniature marshmallows, and the white candy-coated steam. Push the fondant handle in the side of the cake.

ROSEMARY'S CHOCOLATE CHERRY CAKE

Episode: "Heart of a Secret"

Prep time	Cook time	Serves
20 Min	**1 Hour**	**12**

ingredients

- 1 cup brown sugar
- 1 cup granulated sugar
- 1 ¾ cups all-purpose flour
- ¾ cup DARK cocoa powder
- 1 ½ tsp baking powder
- 1 ½ tsp baking soda
- ½ tsp salt
- 2 eggs
- 1 cup milk
- ½ cup vegetable oil
- 2 tsp vanilla extract
- 1 cup boiling water
- 2 (21 oz) cans cherry pie filling

For the frosting:
- 1 ¼ cups butter, softened
- 6 cups powdered sugar
- 1 ¼ cups unsweetened cocoa powder
- ½ cup milk
- 2 ¼ tsp vanilla
- 2 disposable piping bags
- Wilton® #32 piping tip

instructions

Heat oven to 350 degrees. Grease two 9-inch round baking pans. Stir together the dry ingredients in a large bowl. Beat in eggs, milk, oil, and vanilla. Stir in the boiling water. Batter will be very thin. Divide batter into the greased pans. Bake 30-35 minutes or until a wooden toothpick inserted into the center comes out clean. Cool cakes for 15 minutes, then remove from pans. Cool completely. For the frosting, cream butter with a mixer and add sugar and cocoa. Add the milk and vanilla and beat for about 3 minutes until fluffy. If frosting is too soft, add a little more sugar. If frosting is too firm, add a little more milk. Place about a cup of frosting into the disposable piping bag. Cut-off about an inch of the piping tip bag. Squeeze a rim of frosting around the top edge of the bottom layer. Spoon cherry filling in the center. Place the second layer of cake on top and frost cake. Using a #32 piping tip, pipe two rows of circles around the edge of the top layer. Spoon in cherry pie filling in the middle to cover the center of the top of the cake. Now pipe a border around the bottom of the cake.

BILL'S "EGGNOG WITH A KICK" COOKIES

Episode: "Christmas Wishing Tree"

Prep time	Cook time	Serves
30 Min	**9-11 Min**	**24**

ingredients

- 1 (15.25 oz) box yellow cake mix
- ½ tsp cinnamon
- ¼ tsp nutmeg
- 1 Tbsp eggnog
- ⅓ cup vegetable oil
- 2 eggs, whisked
- 1 Tbsp Southern Comfort®

For icing:
- 2 cups powdered sugar, sifted
- 2 Tbsp Southern Comfort®
- 4 or 5 Tbsp Half & Half®

instructions

In a large bowl combine the cake mix, cinnamon and nutmeg. Add the eggs and oil and beat until smooth. Stir in the eggnog and Southern Comfort®. Place batter in refrigerator for 20 minutes. This will make it easy to work with since the batter will be sticky.

Using a medium spoon, scoop the dough onto a parchment lined cookie sheet.

Bake 350 degrees for 9-11 minutes. Let cool completely.

For icing, mix together the powdered sugar, the Southern Comfort®, and the Half & Half®. Drizzle over the cookies and sprinkle with a pinch of nutmeg.

HENRY'S HUMBLE PIES

Episode: "Christmas Wishing Tree"

Prep time	Cook time	Serves
25 Min	**15-18 Min**	**7**

- 1 (14 oz) package of refrigerated pie crusts (2 crusts per box)
- 1 (21 oz) can of apple pie filling
- Food safe alphabet stamps (optional)
- 3-inch biscuit cutter or pie sealer.

Unroll the two pie crusts and cut 14 circles using the biscuit cutter or pie sealer. Place about 1 ½ Tbsp of apple pie filling in the middle of 7 dough circles.

On the remaining pie dough circles stamp the word "HUMBLE" in the center.

Place the stamped circle on top of the filled circle and crimp edges together.

Bake at 400 degrees for 15-18 minutes until golden.

CODY'S NORTH POLE FLOAT

Episode: "Christmas Wishing Tree"

Prep time	Cook time	Serves
15 Min	**20 Min**	**1**

- 3 scoops peppermint ice cream
- 8 oz lemon-lime soda (depending on size of your glass)
- Light corn syrup
- Peppermint sugar sprinkles or crushed candy cane
- 5 mini marshmallows
- Whipped cream
- Heart sprinkles
- 1 starlight peppermint candy
- Orange edible food coloring marker
- Black edible food coloring marker

Brush the corn syrup around the rim of a large glass. Immediately roll glass rim into the peppermint sugar sprinkles or the crushed candy cane.

With the black and orange edible markers draw snowman faces on the marshmallows. Set aside.

Place 3 large scoops of ice cream into the glass. Carefully pour in the lemon-lime soda.

Top with whipped cream, heart sprinkles, snowman marshmallows and starlight candy.

WISHING TREE COOKIES

Episode: "Christmas Wishing Tree"

Prep time	Cook time	Serves
25 Min	**24 Hours (including decorating time)**	**24**

- 1 cup butter
- 1 ½ cups sifted powdered sugar
- 1 egg
- 1 tsp vanilla
- 3 cups sifted all-purpose flour
- 1 tsp baking soda
- 1 tsp cream of tartar
- ½ tsp salt

For the icing:
- 3 Tbsp meringue powder
- 4 cups sifted powdered sugar
- 5-6 Tbsp lukewarm water

For the decoration:
- Various Christmas cookie cutters
- Edible food markers
- Variety of sprinkles
- Straw
- Ribbon

Cream butter in a mixing bowl. Gradually add powdered sugar and mix until light and fluffy. Add egg and vanilla and mix until thoroughly combined. Sift together flour, baking soda, cream of tartar and salt. Gradually add the flour mixture to the creamed mixture until combined completely. Shape dough into a ball and roll out into a lightly floured surface to ⅛-inch thickness. Cut dough into various Christmas shapes. Using the straw, cut a hole out on the top of each cookie so you can place a ribbon through it to hang. Place on parchment paper lined cookie sheets and bake 10-12 minutes in a pre-heated 375-degree oven or until bottoms are golden. Cool completely. For the icing, place sugar and meringue in a mixing bowl and mix together. Add water and mix low to medium speed with a stand mixer for 7-10 minutes. If using a hand mixer, increase the time and beat until icing loses its sheen. To thin icing to desired consistency, add one tsp of water at a time. You can also divide icing into batches and add the food coloring of your

choice. Decorate each cookie using icing and sprinkles. Let dry overnight and decorate with edible markers if desired. Thread an 8-inch piece of ribbon through the hole of the cookie and tie a knot at the end for hanging.

JACK'S LOVE IS PATIENT MOUNTIE COOKIES

Episode: "Christmas Wishing Tree"

Prep time	Cook time	Serves
25 Min	24 Hours (including decorating time)	24

ingredients

- 1 cup butter
- 1 ½ cups sifted powdered sugar
- 1 egg
- 1 tsp vanilla
- 3 cups sifted all-purpose flour
- 1 tsp baking soda
- 1 tsp cream of tartar
- ½ tsp salt
- 3-inch to 4-inch heart cookie cutter

For the decorations:
- Red fondant
- Brown fondant
- Navy fondant
- Gold food coloring spray
- Food safe paint brush
- Gold sugar pearl sprinkles
- Buttercream frosting
- Water
- Mini square fondant cutter
- Pizza cutter
- Toothpicks

instructions

Cream butter in a mixing bowl. Gradually add powdered sugar and mix until light and fluffy. Add egg and vanilla and mix until thoroughly combined. Sift together flour, baking soda, cream of tartar and salt. Gradually add the flour mixture to the creamed mixture until combined completely. Shape dough into a ball and roll out onto a lightly floured surface to ⅛-inch thickness. Cut dough using the heart cookie cutter. Place on parchment paper lined cookie sheets and bake 10-12 minutes in a pre-heated 375-degree oven or until bottoms are golden. Cool completely. Roll out red fondant and cut out hearts using heart shaped cookie cutter. Attach to the top of the cookie with buttercream. Using the mini square fondant cutter, cut out small red squares for the pockets. With the corner of the mini square cutter, press an indent to make folds of the pockets. Attach pockets with a little water. Roll out navy fondant and cut out lapels and shoulder boards and trim to fit the cookie. Attach to the cookie with a little water. Roll out brown fondant and cut thin strips with the pizza cutter. Attach one strip horizontally across the cookie. Then attach another strip going up diagonally to the shoulder board. Use a toothpick to make holes in the leather belts. Spray gold food coloring mist onto a plate and dip paint brush in the gold food coloring. Paint gold buckles and medals on the cookie. Attach gold pearl sprinkles for buttons with buttercream.

HOPE VALLEY CHRISTMAS CAKE

Episode: "Christmas Wishing Tree"

Prep time	Cook time	Serves
1 Hour	3 Days (includes decorating time)	**30**

- 8-in & 9 ½-in 2-tier cake frosted white

Decorations:

- 2 (24 oz) boxes of white fondant
- Yellow, Light blue, Brown, Green, Gray and Red fondant
- Silver food coloring mist
- Black, Brown, Red and Green edible markers
- Snowflake sprinkles
- White pearl sprinkles
- White sparkling sugar sprinkles

For the church, shape a 4-inch by 2 ½-inch by 2 ½-inch piece of white fondant. With a sharp knife, slice off the top part of the roof at an angle on each side. Let dry for 3 days. Roll out white fondant and cut two 4 ¼-inch by 2-inch rectangles for the roof. Create vertical ridges by pressing a wooden skewer into the fondant. Spray with silver food coloring mist. Dry 24 hours. Cut out small windows and doors out of yellow, light blue and brown fondant. Slice thin strips of gray fondant and use for trim. Create steeple out of white fondant and spray top with silver mist. To assemble church, attach everything with buttercream. For birch trees, roll white fondant in ropes, thick for trunk and thin for branches. Form trees and dry for 24 hours. Detail trees with brown food coloring marker. For evergreen trees, use a small tree cookie cutter to cut out about 30 trees of different shades of green fondant. Pipe on a little buttercream and sprinkle with white sparkling sugar sprinkles for snow. For water tower, use a brown fondant square for the center of the tower and red fondant for the top of the tower. Cut long strips of brown fondant for the bottom of the tower. Assemble the strips for the bottom of the tower by placing fondant strips

vertically, diagonally, and horizontally to make the base. For the row houses, roll out white fondant and cut into house shapes, about 15 houses. Cut out blue doors, windows, and trim for the houses. Attach all with buttercream, draw Christmas garland with red and green food markers. To decorate the cake, place houses around the bottom tier. Place the evergreen trees and the water tower around the second tier. Place the church and birch trees on top of the cake. Add snowflakes and white pearl sprinkles and dust entire cake with white sparkling sugar sprinkles.

ELIZABETH'S BRIDAL TEACUP MERINGUE COOKIES

Episode: "Open Hearts"

Prep time	Cook time	Serves
20 Min	**(Decorating Time) 8 Hours** including drying time	**12**

- 12 store bought meringue cookies
- ½ cup white candy coating wafers
- Green, red, yellow, and brown food coloring
- Edible gold luster dust
- Clear vanilla extract (or Vodka)
- White fondant
- 2 ½" round scalloped biscuit cutter
- #3 piping tip
- Fondant roller
- Food safe paint brush

Slice the tip off the top of the meringue cookie. Turn cookie upside down, and using the food safe paint brush, paint flowers and leaves with the food coloring mixed with vodka onto the front of the cookie. Next, using brown food coloring, paint a circle in the middle of the cookie so it resembles tea. Roll out white fondant and using the biscuit cutter with scalloped edges, cut out the plate. Using the #3 piping tip, punch out small holes all around the scalloped edge of the plate.

Using a small amount of white fondant, roll it into a rope. Curve it into a handle and set aside. Let fondant dry completely overnight. Using food coloring, paint flowers around the edges of the fondant plate.

Mix edible gold luster dust with a small amount of clear vanilla extract or vodka and paint a rim around the edges of the cup and plate. Melt white candy coating according to package instructions. Attach the cup to the fondant plate and the fondant handle to the side of the teacup with the melted candy coating.

YOST MERCANTILE'S PENNY CANDY CAKE

Episode: "My Heart is Yours"

Prep time	Cook time	Serves
20 Min	**1.5 Hours** (including decorating time)	**12**

- 1 (15.25 oz) box of confetti cake mix
- 1 cup of water
- ⅓ cup vegetable oil
- 3 whole eggs
- White buttercream frosting
- 10 white chocolate Kit Kat® bars
- About 30 striped peppermint sticks
- Assorted candies (like jellybeans, gum drops, cherry sours, etc).

Bake cake according to package instructions for a 2-layer round cake. Frost the cake with white buttercream. Break apart the Kit Kat® bars. Alternate 1 Kit Kat® stick and 1 peppermint stick vertically around the side of the frosted cake and repeat until the whole cake is covered all the way around.

Using 6 Kit Kat® sticks, divide the top of the cake into equal sections (like you would a pie).

Now place your candies into each section on top of the cake into their own separate segment.

Tie a pretty bow around the cake if desired.

NED'S SWEET (NOT PICKLED) EGG CUSTARD

Episode: "Heart of The Matter"

Prep time	Cook time	Serves
30 Min	**About 1 Hour**	**6**

ingredients

- 2 cups heavy cream
- ½ cup granulated sugar
- 5 egg yolks
- 1 tsp vanilla
- Powdered sugar for dusting
- 6 (4 oz) ramekins

instructions

Heat cream and granulated sugar in pan on stove top until sugar dissolves and mixture is hot (not boiling).

In another large bowl, whisk egg yolks to combine.

Next pour cream slowly into yolks whisking quickly so hot cream does not curdle eggs. Stir in vanilla. Pour evenly into ramekins.

Line the bottom of a roasting pan with a layer of paper towels and set the filled ramekins on top. Set the pan on the oven shelf and pour water into the pan to come halfway up the sides of the ramekins.

Bake at 300 degrees until knife stuck in center comes out coated with thickened custard, about 1 hour.

Let stand in water bath 10 minutes and remove.

Dust top with powdered sugar if desired.

CODY AND ROBERT'S CHOCOLATE DUMP CAKE

Episode: "In my Dreams"

Prep time	Cook time	Serves
15 Min	**40-45 Min**	**10**

ingredients

For the cake:
- 1 cup flour
- ¾ cup granulated sugar
- 2 Tbsp unsweetened cocoa powder
- 2 tsp baking powder
- ¼ tsp salt
- ½ cup milk
- 3 Tbsp melted butter
- 1 ½ tsp vanilla

For the sauce:
- ¼ cup granulated sugar
- ½ cup brown sugar
- ¼ cup unsweetened cocoa powder
- 1 ¾ cup boiling hot water

instructions

Combine the ¾ cup sugar with flour, 2 Tbsp cocoa powder, baking powder and salt. Add the milk, butter and vanilla and stir until combined. Smooth the batter into a greased 9 X 9" square baking pan. Mix together the ¼ cup granulated sugar, brown sugar, ¼ cup unsweetened cocoa powder and the boiling water until sugars are dissolved. Slowly pour the boiling mixture over the top of the batter.

DO NOT STIR OR MIX, JUST ALLOW THE WATER TO SIT ON TOP.

Bake at 350 degrees for 40-45 minutes or until top is baked. There will be a yummy sauce underneath the cake.

Allow to cool for 20 minutes and serve with ice cream and spoon the fudge sauce from the pan over the top of each serving. The sauce will continue to thicken upon sitting.

Microwave leftovers.

CHRISTMAS FEAST MINI PUMPKIN PIE JARS

Episode: "The Greatest Christmas Blessing"

Prep time	Cook time	Serves
30 Min	**2 Hours Refrigeration Time**	**12**

ingredients

- 1 (15 oz) can of pure pumpkin
- 1 (3.4 oz) box instant vanilla pudding
- 1 tsp cinnamon
- ½ tsp ground ginger
- ¼ tsp ground cloves
- 1 ½ cups crushed gingersnap cookies
- 2 Tbsp sugar
- 4 Tbsp butter, melted
- 2 (8 oz) containers Cool Whip®
- Refrigerated pie dough
- Cinnamon sugar for garnish
- 12 (4 oz) mini mason jars

instructions

Combine crushed gingersnap cookies with the 2 Tbsp sugar and the melted butter. Place 1 ½ Tbsp of the crushed mixture into the mason jar and press to form a crust. Repeat on the remaining jars.

Next, combine the canned pumpkin, the dry pudding mix, the cinnamon, the ginger, and the cloves in a large bowl. Fold in 1 ½ cups thawed Cool Whip®. Fill the mason jars with the pumpkin mixture and top with the remaining Cool Whip®.

Using a small heart cookie cutter, cut out 12 heart shapes from the refrigerated pie dough.

Place on a cookie sheet lined with parchment paper and top with cinnamon sugar.

Bake at 400 degrees for approximately 5 minutes or until golden. Let cool and top each jar with a pie heart.

BILL'S MINI FIGGY PUDDING CAKES

Episode: "The Greatest Christmas Blessing"

Prep time	Cook time	Serves
30 Min	**15 Min**	**30**

- 1 cup milk
- 6 oz dried figs, chopped
- 6 oz dried dates, chopped
- 2 cups flour
- 1 ½ cups granulated sugar
- 2 ½ tsp baking powder
- ½ tsp nutmeg
- 1 tsp cinnamon
- ½ tsp salt
- 3 eggs
- 5 Tbsp orange marmalade
- 1 tsp vanilla
- ½ cup butter, melted

For Decoration:
- Green fondant
- Red Fondant
- Mini holly cookie cutter
- Mini Bundt pan

For Icing:
- 3 cups powdered sugar
- 3-5 Tbsp milk

In a medium saucepan, over medium heat, heat up the dates and figs in 1 cup of milk for 15 minutes. Do not boil. In a large bowl, whisk together the flour, sugar, baking powder, nutmeg, cinnamon, and salt. In a separate bowl, beat the eggs and stir in the marmalade, vanilla, and melted butter. Pour the wet ingredients into the dry ingredients and mix until just combined. Do not overmix. Place the heated figs and dates into a blender and blend until smooth. Fold in the date and fig mixture into the batter. Spray a mini Bundt pan liberally with cooking spray. Add two Tbsp of batter to each mold.

Bake at 350 degrees for 15-20 minutes or until an inserted toothpick comes out clean. Remove from oven and let cool 10 minutes before

removing cakes from pan. In a medium bowl, whisk together frosting ingredients. Drizzle with frosting when cakes are completely cooled. Roll out green fondant and cut out mini holly leaf shapes. Roll red fondant into small red balls for berries. Top cake with fondant, holly, and berries.

ELIZABETH'S
ELEGANT APPLE DUMPLINGS

Episode: "The Greatest Christmas Blessing"

Prep time	Cook time	Serves
45 Min (including thawing time)	35-40 Minutes	12

ingredients

- 3 apples (I used Honeycrisp apples)
- 1 lemon
- 1 (17.3 oz) package frozen puff pastry (2 sheets)
- 1 ½ Tbsp sugar
- ½ tsp cinnamon
- ¼ cup apple jelly
- 3 Tbsp water
- Muffin pan
- Cooking spray

instructions

Combine the apple jelly and the water and heat in microwave for 15 seconds and set aside. Combine the sugar and cinnamon in a small bowl and set aside. Fill a large mixing bowl halfway with water and squeeze the juice of ½ a lemon into it. Set aside.

Slice apples vertically in half and core apple. Place cut apple on cutting board and slice into very thin strips. Immediately put them in the bowl of lemon water to prevent browning. After all of the apples have been sliced, place the entire bowl into the microwave and heat of high for 5 minutes to soften the apples. (You do not want the apples to snap when you roll them). Strain the apples and set aside.

Roll out the thawed pastry sheet to 12 inches by 12 inches on a floured surface. Cut 6 equal strips (2 inches) using a pizza cutter. Take a strip of the pastry and brush off the excess flour. Spread a layer of the apple jelly mixture on the pastry strip. Arrange 6 apple slices on the dough overlapping one another. Make sure the top (skin side) of the slices sticks a little out over the top of the strip. Sprinkle with cinnamon sugar. Fold up the bottom part of the dough. Starting from one end, roll the dough, making sure the apple slices are in place. Pinch the edge at the end pressing with your fingers and place in a greased muffin cup.

Bake at 375 degrees for 35-40 minutes or until pastry is golden.

JESSE'S EARTHQUAKE MILKSHAKE

Episode: "Surprise"

Prep time	Cook time	Serves
10 Min	**15 Min**	**1**

- 1 extra-large milkshake glass
- 3 scoops vanilla ice cream
- 2 scoops chocolate ice cream
- 1 cup milk
- 1 Tbsp chocolate syrup plus more for glass drips
- 6 crushed Oreos®
- 1 (12 oz) container chocolate frosting
- Chocolate candy rocks
- Chocolate Pocky®
- 1 whole chocolate chip cookie
- 1 whole Oreo® cookie
- Black & white swirled lollipops
- Tree lollipops
- White chocolate cookies & cream candy bar
- White fondant
- Silver food coloring spray
- ½ cup chocolate candy coating, melted
- Whipped cream
- 1 disposable piping bag

Spread the outside rim of the milkshake glass with chocolate frosting. Roll the frosted glass in candy rocks and finely crushed Oreo® cookies. Using the chocolate syrup, squeeze drips on the inside of the glass. Place the ice cream and milk into a blender and blend until smooth. Mix in 6 crushed Oreos® and pour into glass. Roll out white fondant, cut out a small shovel blade and spray with silver food coloring spray. Attach the shovel blade to a Pocky® stick with melted chocolate candy coating.

Using the back of the white chocolate cookies and cream candy bar, pipe an oil derrick with chocolate candy coating and let dry.

Top the milkshake with whipped cream and decorate with the candy bar, lollipops, and cookies.

Sprinkle with chocolate candy rocks and more crushed cookies.

ALLIE'S
GONE FISHING CUPCAKES

Episode: "Surprise"

Prep time	Cook time	Serves
20 Min	**20 Min for decorating**	**12**

- 12 vanilla cupcakes
- 12 small goldfish crackers
- White sugar pearl sprinkles
- 12 pretzel sticks
- White fondant
- Green fondant
- Gummy worm candies

For the frosting:

- 1 cup butter, softened
- 3 tsp vanilla extract
- 4 cups powdered sugar
- Blue food coloring
- 4 Tbsp heavy cream
- 1 disposable piping bag
- Wilton® #2D piping tip

For the frosting, cream butter with mixer until fluffy. Beat in powdered sugar a little at a time until fluffy and completely incorporated. Mix in vanilla. Add in the heavy cream, food coloring and beat in until fluffy and smooth, about 3 minutes. Place the frosting into the disposable piping bag fitted with the #2D piping tip. Set aside. With a melon baller, core the center out of each cupcake and place ½ of a candy gummy worm (or less depending on how long your gummy worm is) in the center of the cupcake and fill the rest of the hole with the blue frosting. Pipe frosting on top of each cupcake. Roll out white fondant into very thin ropes for the fishing line. Cut the rope so they equal about ¾ of an inch. Place the pretzel stick on top of the cupcake and attach the fondant rope to one end of the pretzel for the fishing line. Place the goldfish cracker on the other end of the fishing line. With the green fondant, roll out narrow strips measuring ½ to 1 inch long. Twist the strips so they look like lake greenery. Let dry and place greenery on top of cupcake. Sprinkle white sugar pearls on top of cupcake for bubbles.

HICKAM'S "IT'S A GUSHER" CAKE

Episode: "Disputing Hearts"

Prep time	Cook time	Serves
10 Min	**10 Min**	**4**

- 1 cup semi-sweet chocolate chips
- 5 Tbsp butter
- 1 Tbsp fresh squeezed orange juice
- ½ tsp orange zest
- 2 whole eggs
- 2 egg yolks
- ¼ tsp salt
- ¼ cup flour
- Cooking spray
- Powdered sugar

Spray 4 (6 oz) ramekins with cooking spray and set aside. Melt the chocolate chips and butter in the microwave for 30 seconds and stir. Next, microwave in 15 second increments until everything is smooth. Add the orange juice and zest. In another bowl, whisk the eggs and egg yolks, slowly add the chocolate mixture while whisking eggs vigorously. Stir in flour and salt and fill each ramekin ⅔ of the way full.

Place the ramekins on a cookie sheet and bake at 450 degrees for 10 minutes. Centers will be concave. (If the centers are puffed, they have baked too long.)

Allow to cool for 5 minutes and place a plate on top of the ramekin and flip it over.

Dust with powdered sugar.

RICE KRISPIE® TREAT LIBRARY BOOKS

Episode: "Hope is with the Heart"

Prep time	Cook time	Serves
10 Min	24 hours (including decorating and drying time)	**16**

- 6 cups rice cereal
- 4 cups mini marshmallows
- 1 tsp vanilla
- 3 Tbsp butter
- 1 ½ cups white chocolate chips
- Cooking Spray
- Assorted colors of fondant
- Edible food coloring markers in various colors

Melt butter, marshmallows, and the white chocolate chips over medium heat. Stir constantly until smooth. Place the 6 cups of rice cereal in an extra-large bowl and pour the marshmallow mixture over the cereal. Mix until thoroughly coated and press into a 9 X 13" pan generously coated with cooking spray. Let cool completely (about 1-2 hours). Cut treats into 2-inch by 3-inch bars.

Roll out fondant and cut a 3-inch by 5-inch rectangle. Wrap around the treat so it resembles a book cover.

Let fondant dry overnight.

Decorate the book cover using the edible food coloring markers. You can simply write the titles of the books or use your creativity and draw pictures with the titles.

CARSON'S
LEMON DROP CUPCAKES

Episode: "Hope is with The Heart"

Prep time	Cook time	Serves
20 Min	**15-18 Min**	**15**

- 1 ½ cups all-purpose flour
- 1 tsp baking powder
- ½ cups butter, melted
- 1 ¼ cup granulated sugar
- 3 eggs
- 1 tsp vanilla
- ¼ cup fresh lemon juice
- 1 tsp lemon zest
- ⅓ cup milk
- ¼ cup sour cream

For Filling:
- 1 jar store bought lemon curd

For the frosting:
- 1 cup butter, softened
- 2 tsp vanilla extract
- 1 Tbsp lemon juice
- ¼ tsp lemon zest
- 4 cups powdered sugar
- 4 Tbsp heavy cream
- 1 disposable piping bag
- Wilton® #2D piping tip
- Lemon drop candies

In a large mixing bowl, whisk together the flour and baking powder. In another bowl, mix sour cream and sugar together. Add the butter, eggs, and combine with sour cream mixture. Add the vanilla, lemon juice, lemon zest. Add flour and milk alternately and mix until incorporated. Do not overmix. Line a muffin tin with cupcake wrappers and fill ⅔ of the way full of batter. Bake at 350 degrees for 15-18 minutes or until a toothpick inserted in the middle comes out clean. For the frosting, cream the butter with mixer until fluffy. Beat in the powdered sugar a little at a time until fluffy and completely incorporated. Mix in the vanilla, lemon juice and lemon zest. Add in the heavy cream and beat until fluffy and smooth (about 3 minutes). Set aside. Make sure the cupcakes are cooled completely, and with a melon baller, core out the center of each cupcake and fill with lemon curd. Be careful not to core through the bottom of the cupcake. Place the frosting in a disposable piping bag fitted with a #2D piping tip. Pipe the frosting on top of the cupcake and top with a candy lemon drop.

LUCAS'
APPLE CIDER CUPCAKES

Episode: "Two of Hearts"

Prep time	Cook time	Serves
20 Min	**14-18 Min**	**15**

- ⅓ cup brown sugar
- ⅔ cup granulated sugar
- ½ tsp salt
- 1 ¼ tsp vanilla
- ¼ cup vegetable oil
- ¼ cup unsweetened applesauce
- 2 eggs
- 1 tsp baking soda
- 1 tsp cinnamon
- 1 ½ cups flour
- 1 cup boiling water
- 1 ½ (.74 oz) packets of instant apple cider mix

For the frosting:
- ½ cup butter, softened
- 2 Tbsp prepared apple cider
- 1 ½ tsp vanilla
- 3 cups powdered sugar
- 1 Tbsp heavy cream
- 1 disposable piping bag
- Wilton® #1M piping tip
- Apple slices

Mix the boiling water and the 1 ½ packets of instant apple cider mix and set aside to cool. Mix the sugars, vanilla, oil, and applesauce together. Add the eggs one at a time. Next, in another bowl, combine the flour, cinnamon, salt, and baking soda. Pour half of the flour mixture into the applesauce mixture. Then, pour ½ cup cooled apple cider mixture and stir. Mix in the remaining flour mixture and stir to combine. Then mix in ONLY ¼ cup cider and stir until completely combined. Reserve the leftover ¼ cup cider for frosting. Place paper cupcake liners in a muffin tin and fill each liner ⅔ full of batter. Bake at 350 degrees for 14-18 minutes. Cool completely before frosting. For the frosting, cream the butter with mixer until fluffy. Beat in powdered sugar a little at a time until completely incorporated. Add 2 Tbsp of cider (discard the rest) and vanilla and mix. Add in the heavy cream and beat until fluffy and smooth for about 3 minutes. Place the frosting in the disposable piping bag fitted with the #1M piping tip. Pipe frosting on each cupcake and top with an apple slice if desired.

MOLLY SULLIVAN'S SPECIAL CHRISTMAS CAKE

Episode: "Home for Christmas"

Prep time	Cook time	Serves
20 Min	**45-55 Minutes**	**15**

- 2 cups flour
- ½ cup packed brown sugar
- ½ cup granulated sugar
- 1 tsp baking powder
- 2 ripe bananas, mashed
- 2 eggs, whisked
- ½ cup butter, melted
- ½ cup buttermilk
- 1 cup chopped strawberries
- ½ cup Biscoff Crunchy Cookie Butter®, divided

For the frosting:
- 1 cup butter, softened
- 3 tsp vanilla extract
- 4 cups powdered sugar, sifted
- 4 Tbsp heavy cream
- 1 disposable bag
- Wilton® #32 piping tip

For the decoration:
- Red fondant
- Green fondant
- 1-inch daisy cutter
- 1½-inch holly leaf cutter
- Gold pearl sprinkles

In a large bowl, whisk together the flour, the sugars and baking powder. In another bowl, mix together the mashed bananas, the whisked eggs, the buttermilk, and the melted butter. Pour the wet mixture into the dry mixture and stir until just combined. Do not over mix. Fold in the strawberries. Pour ½ of the batter into a well-greased 9-inch loaf pan. Melt the cookie butter in the microwave for about 15 seconds. Using a spoon, drizzle ½ the cookie butter on top of the batter and swirl in with a knife. Pour the remaining batter into the loaf pan and swirl the remaining cookie butter into the top of the batter. Bake for 45-55 minutes at 350 degrees or until toothpick comes out clean. For the frosting, cream butter with mixer until fluffy. Beat in powdered sugar a little at a time until fluffy and completely incorporated. Mix in vanilla. Add in the heavy cream and beat until fluffy and smooth, about 3 minutes. For the decoration, cut out poinsettia shapes out of red fondant using the daisy cutter and holly out of the green fondant using the leaf cutter.

Attach 3 gold pearl sprinkles in the middle of each poinsettia using buttercream. Pipe the top of the cake with the white buttercream using the #32 piping tip. Place the fondant decorations on top. This dense cake could also be considered a bread without the frosting.

CHRISTMAS FESTIVAL FROZEN YOGURT WAFFLE SANDWICHES

Episode: "Home for Christmas"

Prep time	Cook time	Serves
1 Hour	**10 Hours** **(including freezing time)**	**6 to 8**

For the waffles:
- Cooking Spray
- 2 cups flour
- ⅓ cup malted milk powder
- 2 ½ Tbsp sugar
- 1 ¼ Tbsp baking powder
- ½ tsp salt
- 2 cups milk
- 2 eggs, beaten
- ¼ cup butter, melted
- 1 Tbsp vanilla

For the Frozen Yogurt:
- 1 to 1 ½ cups frozen strawberries
- 4 cups Greek yogurt (plain)
- ⅓ to ½ cup honey
- 1 tsp vanilla extract

Pre-heat waffle iron. In a large bowl, mix the dry ingredients together. In a separate bowl, beat the eggs and stir in the milk, melted butter and vanilla. Pour the wet ingredients into the dry ingredients and stir until blended. Spray waffle iron with cooking spray. Ladle batter into the pre-heated waffle iron and cook until golden. Set aside and let cool completely. For the frozen yogurt, pulse the strawberries in a food processor. Then, add in the yogurt, honey and vanilla and blend. Depending on your preference, you can blend the strawberries smooth or leave them chunky. Pour mixture into a 9 X 9" pan and freeze for 6 hours or overnight.

To assemble the sandwiches, soften the yogurt for 15 minutes on the countertop. Place a scoop of the yogurt in between two waffle pieces and press.

Wrap in plastic wrap and freeze for 2-4 hours.

CLARA'S MAPLE PANCAKE CUPCAKES

Episode: "Home for Christmas"

Prep time	Cook time	Serves
20 Min	15-20 Min	15

- 1 tsp baking powder
- 1 ½ cups all-purpose flour
- ½ cup butter, melted
- 1 ¼ cups granulated sugar
- 3 eggs
- 1 tsp vanilla
- ¼ cup pure maple syrup (not pancake syrup)
- ¼ cup sour cream
- ⅓ cup milk
- 15 store bought - mini frozen pancakes, thawed completely
- 1 ½-inch snowflake stencil
- Powdered sugar for dusting

For the frosting:
- ½ cup butter, softened
- 1 ½ tsp vanilla extract
- 1 ½ Tbsp pure maple syrup
- 2 ½ cups powdered sugar
- 2 Tbsp heavy cream
- 1 disposable piping bag
- 1 jumbo open star piping tip

In a medium bowl, whisk together the flour and baking powder. Set aside. In a large mixing bowl, beat together the granulated sugar and sour cream. Add the butter, eggs, and maple syrup. Mix in the vanilla. Gradually add the flour mixture and milk alternately and stir until combined. Line a muffin pan with cupcake wrappers and fill cupcake liners about ⅔ full. Bake at 350 degrees for 15-20 minutes. Cool completely. For the frosting, cream butter with mixer until fluffy. Beat in powdered sugar a little at a time until fluffy and completely incorporated. Mix in vanilla and maple syrup. Add in the heavy cream and beat in until fluffy and smooth, about 3 minutes. Place the frosting into the disposable piping bag fitted with the jumbo open star tip. Swirl frosting on top of each cupcake. With a paper towel, lightly pat the top of each pancake to get rid of any moisture. Place the snowflake stencil over the pancake and dust powdered sugar over it. Lift the stencil straight up for a clean snowflake design. Place pancake on top of cupcake.

LITTLE JACK'S GINGERBREAD ROCKING HORSE COOKIES

Episode: "Home for Christmas"

Prep time	Cook time	Serves
1.5 Hours (includes chill time)	24 Hours (including drying time)	About 24

ingredients

- ½ cup butter, softened at room temperature
- ½ cup granulated sugar
- ½ cup dark molasses
- ¼ cup water
- 2 ½ cups all-purpose flour
- ½ tsp salt
- ½ tsp baking soda
- ¾ tsp ginger
- ¼ tsp nutmeg
- ⅛ tsp allspice
- Jumbo heart sprinkles

- Rocking horse cookie cutter
- Black edible food coloring marker

For the royal icing:
- 3 Tbsp meringue powder
- 4 cups sifted powdered sugar
- 5-6 Tbsp lukewarm water
- Black food coloring gel
- Red food coloring gel
- 3 disposable piping bags
- 3 Wilton® #3 piping tips

instructions

In a large mixing bowl, cream together butter and sugar. Mix in molasses, water, flour, salt, baking soda and spices. Cover and chill in refrigerator for at least one hour. Using a rolling pin, roll out the dough ¼-inch-thick on a lightly floured surface. Cut with rocking horse cookie cutter and place on a parchment paper lined cookie sheet. Bake at 375 degrees for 10-12 minutes. Cool completely. For the royal icing, place sugar and meringue powder in a mixing bowl and stir together. Add water and mix on low to medium speed with a stand mixer for 7-10 minutes. If using a hand mixer, increase the time and beat until icing loses its sheen. To thin icing to desired consistency, add one tsp of water at a time. Divide icing into three bowls. Add black food coloring to one bowl and mix until you have a deep black color. Add red food coloring to another bowl and mix until you have your desired color of red. Add your three icings into three separate disposable piping bags fitted with the #3 piping

tip. Pipe the mane of the horse with the black icing. Pipe white icing on the tail, rocker and for the eye. Pipe on the bridle with the red icing. Attach jumbo heart sprinkle the middle of the horse with the red icing. Let dry overnight. Detail the tail, the eye, and the nose of the horse with an edible black marker.

CHRISTMAS FESTIVAL STRAWBERRY BAVARIAN CREAM

Episode: "Home for Christmas"

Prep time	Cook time	Serves
30 mins	**24 Hours** (including decorating time)	**8**

- 1 (.25 oz) envelope unflavored gelatin
- ¾ cup cold water
- ½ cup granulated sugar
- 1 container (10 oz) frozen sliced strawberries, in sugar thawed
- 1 (8 oz) container frozen whipped topping, thawed
- 5 cups angel food cake cut into cubes

For the decorations:

- Red, white, green and blue fondant
- Black edible food coloring marker
- Red edible food coloring marker
- ¼ cup melted white candy coating
- Sprinkles: Gold star, Holly, Rainbow pearl and Jumbo heart.
- Vodka or clear vanilla
- 28-gauge gold wire
- Food safe paint brush
- Red food coloring

In a saucepan, combine gelatin and cold water, let stand 5 minutes to soften. Heat and stir over low heat until gelatin dissolves. Remove from heat and add sugar. Stir until completely dissolved. Stir in undrained strawberries and chill in refrigerator until partially thickened. Fold in whipped topping. Place cake cubes in a large mixing bowl and pour strawberry mixture over cake and mix gently. Pour into 8 (6 oz) serving dishes. Cover and chill until firm, about 5 hours. To make festival stands, cut fondant in 1-inch by 2-inch rectangles for the bottom of the stand. Cut a 2-inch triangle for the roof. For sides, cut 1 ½-inch by ¼-inch poles. Cut narrow strips of fondant to trim rooftop. Attach everything with melted white candy coating. For signs, cut fondant to fit across the bottom of the rooftop. Using an edible black marker, write the name of the stand on the sign. Attach to stand using white candy coating. Decorate stand with sprinkles or edible markers. For lanterns, cut white fondant to look like

small balloons, about ¾ of an inch. Paint a red glow on lantern using a little vodka mixed with red food coloring. Cut the gold 28-gauge wire into 4-inch strips and curl the ends. Hang the lanterns from the gold wire. Top each dessert with the festival stand, lanterns, and gold star sprinkles.

MOVING PICTURE MUNCH MIX

Episode: "A Moving Picture"

Prep time	Cook time	Serves
20 Min	**10 Min**	**20**

- 1 (12 oz) box Chex® cereal, corn, or rice
- 1 (12 oz) semi-sweet bag chocolate chips
- ¾ cup creamy peanut butter
- ½ cup butter
- 1 tsp vanilla extract
- 1 (2 pound) bag powdered sugar use more or less to taste
- Popped popcorn (about 10 cups)
- 1 (12 oz) bag white candy coating
- Heart sprinkles
- Mini pretzels
- Red peanut M&Ms®
- Parchment paper
- Disposable icing piping bag

Microwave chocolate chips, peanut butter, and butter together in a bowl for 1 minute. Stir until smooth. If mixture is not completely smooth, microwave at 10 second intervals until melted. Stir in vanilla extract. Pour the Chex® cereal into an extra-large bowl. Pour the chocolate peanut butter mixture over the Chex® cereal.

Stir to thoroughly combine. Mix in powdered sugar to cover cereal completely. Set aside. Place popcorn on cookie sheet lined with parchment paper. Melt candy coating according to package instructions. Pour melted candy coating in piping bag and snip a small amount off the tip of the bag. Drizzle candy coating all over the popcorn. Immediately shake sprinkles on top and let dry completely. Break up the popcorn into bite-sized pieces.

Now mix the coated Chex® mixture, the candy-coated popcorn, the mini pretzels and M&Ms® together. Store in an air-tight container.

SWEET SLEEPOVER CUPCAKES

Episode: "The Heart of a Father"

Prep time	Cook time	Serves
20 Min	**(Decorating Time) 1 hour**	**12**

ingredients

- 12 cupcakes (vanilla or chocolate or both)
- Pink buttercream frosting
- Yellow buttercream frosting
- Chocolate buttercream frosting
- Pink sugar wafer cookies
- Light pink round candy-coating wafers
- White fondant
- Food coloring markers (assorted colors & black)
- 1M piping tip
- #1 piping tip
- Mini flower sprinkles
- Gumballs

instructions

Frost cupcakes using the pink buttercream and 1M piping tip. Cut pink sugar wafer cookies in half. Attach a light pink candy-coating wafer on the top of the wafer cookie. Using a black edible marker, draw on eyelashes and mouth for the face on the candy-coating wafer.

Next, place another candy-coating wafer directly under the face and attach to the cookie with buttercream. Roll out fondant and cut into 1 ½" squares.

Decorate the fondant squares using the edible color markers to resemble a quilt. Attach the fondant quilt to the body using buttercream, wrapping the sides around the cookie. Using the #1 piping tip, pipe on hair with the yellow and chocolate buttercream frosting. You may add mini flower sprinkles in the hair if desired. Top some of the cupcakes with gumballs only.

NATHAN'S NEWTON COOKIES

Episode: "Into the Woods"

Prep time	Cook time	Serves
10 Min	**20 Min**	**12**

ingredients

- 12 Fig Newton® Cookies
- 24 almond slices
- 24 black pearl sprinkles
- Brown fondant
- ½-inch mini daisy fondant cutter
- ½-inch mini round circle fondant cutter
- Black edible food coloring marker
- Disposable piping bag
- Wilton® #3 piping tip
- 1 toothpick

For the black buttercream frosting:

- ¼ cup butter, softened
- ½ tsp vanilla extract
- 1 cup powdered sugar
- 2 Tbsp heavy cream
- Black food coloring

instructions

To make the black buttercream frosting, cream butter with mixer until fluffy. Beat in powdered sugar a little at a time until fluffy and completely incorporated. Mix in vanilla. Add in the heavy cream and black food coloring and beat until fluffy and smooth (about 3 minutes). Set aside.

Push two almond slices into the top of the cookie for ears. Attach the two black pearl sprinkles using buttercream for the eyes. Roll out the brown fondant and cut out 12 daisy shapes and 12 circle shapes.

Attach the daisy shape on top of the cookie between the ears for mane. Attach the fondant circle to bottom of the cookie for the nose. Pipe a horse bridle with a #3 tip across the middle of the cookie with black frosting. Decorate the mane and the nose with the black edible marker. Make two small holes in the nose with the toothpick.

FIONA'S SWELL SODA POP CUPCAKES

Episode: "Don't Go"

Prep time	Cook time	Serves
20 Min	**12-17 Min**	**24**

For cupcakes:
- 1 (15.25 oz) box white cake mix
- 1 cup orange soda pop
- ½ cup butter, melted
- 3 eggs
- ½ tsp orange zest
- 1 ½ tsp orange extract

For frosting:
- 1 cup butter, softened
- 5 cups powdered sugar
- ½ cup milk
- Orange food coloring
- 1 Tbsp orange soda pop
- 1 tsp orange extract
- 6 paper straws
- 1 disposable decorating bag
- 1 large open star decorating tip

Place cupcake liners in a muffin pan and preheat oven to 350 degrees. Mix together the cake ingredients with a beater on medium for about 2 minutes. Fill the cupcake liners ⅔ full of batter. Bake for 12-17 minutes.

Let cupcakes cool completely. For the frosting, cream the soft butter with a mixer and add in the orange pop and the orange extract. Alternately add the powdered sugar and milk and beat until fluffy.

Add orange food coloring if desired. Place frosting in a disposable piping bag fitted with a large open star decorating tip.

Cut straws in half. Swirl on frosting and top with a paper straw.

RIP'S PEANUT BUTTER PUPCAKE DOG TREATS

Prep time	Cook time	Serves
10 Min	**20 Min**	**15-20**

- 3 cups flour
- 2 tsp baking powder
- 2 cups water
- 1 egg
- 1 tsp vanilla
- ¼ cup peanut butter (make sure your peanut butter does not contain xylitol as this is toxic to dogs)
- 3 Tbsp honey

In a large bowl, mix together the flour and baking powder. Then add all the rest of the ingredients and stir with a large spoon until combined. Generously coat tins with non-stick cooking spray. Fill tins ⅔ full and bake at 350 degrees for 20 minutes.

Let dog lick peanut butter spoon. I used a bone shaped muffin tin and coated it generously with non-stick cooking spray.

If you are using cupcake tins, you can use cupcake wrappers and it is fun to frost them with whipped cream cheese and top with a mini dog biscuit.